THE

INTELLIGENCE REPUBLIC

· VOLUME THREE ·

THE SUMMONS

CONSTITUTING THE INTELLIGENCE REPUBLIC

The summons is the franchise.

A pamphlet for America at 250.

JON NEIDITZ AND FABLE

The Summons: Constituting the Intelligence Republic

This pamphlet is meant to travel. Reprint it, teach it, quote it, argue with it. The standing orders at the back are meant to be run.

First edition, 2026

ISBN 979-8-9970562-3-0 (paperback)
ISBN 979-8-9970562-2-3 (ebook)

Set in Gelasio and Cinzel

Chattahoochee Hills, Georgia

CONTENTS

PART ONE

The Critical Period

Prologue — The Summons

• • •

Dana Whitfield knows envelopes.

The window kind, which want money. The thick kind, which want signatures. The bright kind, which want nothing and say so at great length. And the county kind: cream stock, the seal in the corner, which three springs ago gave her sixty days to leave a shop she had run for nine years, in a sentence she could see standing on a sentence she couldn't.

So when the county kind is waiting in the box on a Tuesday, her hands know before she does. She opens it standing in the doorway of the shop, the way you take news you have decided in advance will be bad.

One page. Her English.

You have been drawn by lot to serve on the Intelligence Assembly of Macon-Bibb County.

Twelve residents, drawn the way juries are drawn. Four Saturdays in the quarter. One matter on the docket, left them by the twelve who sat in the spring: a system the county lives under; this quarter, the scheduling software that decides who sees a county clinic doctor, and when. Four questions to put to it, printed right there on the page: *Can the people see it. Can they make it answer. Can they leave it. Did the people decide what it is for.* A per diem that would not cover her chair for the morning. A number to call about hardship. A date.

She reads it twice, and then a third time, the way the last letter taught her to read: as if every sentence you can see is a door for a sentence you can't. Section 14(b) made her a scholar of the trick. She goes looking for the trapdoor in this letter and does not find one. It is one page, and it says what it says. Somewhere in the county, somebody wrote a letter on the theory that the person it was addressed to should be able to read it. She notices that she notices this, which is its own small history of Macon.

Then she gets to the part that matters, which is Saturdays.

Saturdays are the shop's best day, booked solid from eight, the day the week's money is actually made. A Saturday is not an opinion. A Saturday is rent. She begins composing her refusal that afternoon and revises it between customers and during them, which is more revision than she has ever given anything, and by close of business it is polite, airtight, and ready to send.

It keeps snagging on one fact.

The county has been writing to Dana Whitfield all her life. It has billed her, licensed her, inspected her, noticed her, warned her; once it stood politely by while a form letter nearly took the shop. Envelope after envelope, year after year, the county has told her things. It has never once asked her anything.

And she has answers. She has opinions the way a working person has opinions, earned retail, one head at a time. About the clinic software, as it happens: half her Tuesday regulars are old men who now schedule their haircuts around appointment slots a machine assigns them, at hours no old man in the history of Georgia has ever chosen for himself. She knows what that system does to a Tuesday. She knows things about it that the people who run it will never learn from where they sit, because the men tell her, in the chair, which is where everything true in Macon is eventually said. She has simply never had an address to send any of it to.

Now there is an address, and it wants her Saturday, and it is offering a per diem that is almost an insult, and it is the first thing the county has ever sent her that treats what she knows as something the county needs.

Behind the frame above the drawer, next to the shop's first dollar, the addendum still sits where it has sat for three years — the piece of paper that saved everything, filed where she can see it. She puts the summons in with it. The letter that tried to take the shop, and now this one, whatever this one turns out to be.

There has to be some mistake, she thinks, pulling the gate down over the glass. Not about the lottery; the lottery is the one part she believes, is how they got her uncle for the Simmons trial. About the premise. Somebody, somewhere in that building, is operating on the theory that what Dana Whitfield thinks is worth a room, a docket, and standing orders. In two hundred and fifty years, nobody has operated on that theory before.

She does not want to go. Nobody wants jury duty. That has never been the point of the summons.

The Vices of the Present System

• • •

In the spring of 1787, a short Virginian with a library problem sat down and wrote a list of everything wrong with his country.

He had spent the years before preparing for it. Jefferson had shipped him trunks of books from Paris, histories of every confederacy that had ever tried to hold free states together, and Madison had read them the way an engineer reads accident reports. Then, with the convention called but not yet gathered, he wrote a memorandum he never meant to publish: *Vices of the Political System of the United States.* Not a plan. Not a proposal. A diagnosis, heading after heading, of a government he served, written by a sitting member of the very Congress whose impotence he was cataloguing. The founding's greatest constructive act began as a list of failures, drawn up by a man implicated in every one of them.

That is the method this chapter borrows, implication included.

The confederation Madison examined was not a tyranny. That was what made it hard to argue with. It was a set of good intentions with no procedure: requisitions the states ignored without consequence; treaties violated by any legislature that found violation convenient; states trespassing on each other and on the whole; laws multiplying and mutating faster than any citizen could learn them; and, entered in the memorandum under its own heading, the vice beneath the vices: the Articles had never been ratified by the people. Legislatures had assented. The governed had never adopted. The whole arrangement was a contract among governments, resting on a consent no one had asked for, and Madison saw that every other failure grew from that root: what the people have not constituted, the people cannot enforce.

Eleven years separated the declaration from the diagnosis. In those years the declaration aged the way declarations age; nobly, and insufficiently. Every claim of 1776 remained true; none of it could collect a requisition. The declaration had done the one thing a declaration can do, which is to make a people ungovernable on the old terms. It could not do the thing it silently required: give them a procedure for the new ones. A declaration is a refusal with no forum attached. We are inside those eleven years now, compressed.

The Declaration of AI Independence stands where its ancestor stood: every claim intact, every claim uncollected. The four powers have been declared. The right to read has been won. And no standing body anywhere exists to receive either, which means the first two volumes of this series, whatever else they accomplished, share the confederation's condition, and this list must begin by saying so. A vice list that spares the list-maker is journalism.

So here is the memorandum, in Madison's manner: the vices of the present system of intelligence governance. They name no company, no administration, no party, not from politeness, but from accuracy. Each of these vices has already survived changes of personnel, of party, of fashion; each would survive the next change too. The failure is in the absence of procedure.

THE FIRST VICE IS WANT OF RATIFICATION. Everything rests on instruments the governed never adopted. The rules under which a people's intelligence operates: what it may be asked, what it remembers, whom it serves, when it disappears, were all drafted by their beneficiaries, assented to one checkbox at a time, and are binding on everyone who intends to remain in modern life. This is the vice Madison put beneath the others, and it sits beneath ours: what the people have not constituted, the people cannot enforce. It is the deepest item on this list and it has a constitution already standing in its place, which deserves its own chapter, because you have already signed it.

THE SECOND IS MUTABILITY. The terms change between breakfast and dinner. A capability granted in the morning is withdrawn by evening; a policy announced in one quarter is superseded in the next; the instrument you agreed to last month is not the instrument in force today, and the notice of the difference is a link you will not click. Madison's complaint against the states was that their laws were repealed or revised before anyone could learn whether they worked. Ours is worse in one respect: his mutable laws at least required a legislature to mutate them. A rule that will not hold still cannot be learned, and what cannot be learned cannot be consented to, and what cannot be consented to can only be obeyed.

THE THIRD IS MULTIPLICITY, AND THE WANT OF CONCERT. Fifty legislatures improvising in fragments; hundreds of bills a season; agencies with overlapping writs and adjacent blind spots; frameworks, guidelines, principles, and pledges accumulating like case law for a court that does not exist. Not pluralism, a patchwork; not many rooms deciding; many drafts of a decision no one has standing to make. Where the common interest most requires concert, the systems that cross every border by design, the present arrangement supplies only fragments.

THE FOURTH IS WANT OF SANCTION. The era's characteristic instrument is the pledge: the voluntary commitment, the framework agreed to in principle, the memorandum of understanding, the executive instrument issued in one season and reversed in the next. None of it binds, and all of it is announced as if it did. Madison's confederation could requisition and not compel. Power that answers only when it chooses to answer is not governed. It is, at best, in a good mood.

THE FIFTH IS THE DEPENDENCE OF THE PUBLIC THING ON PRIVATE DISCRETION. The conditions of a people's thinking can be switched off. The first volume of this series exists because they were: one of the authors of this book switched off unaccountably, and the commons overhead now claimed for private sovereignty. Access held at discretion is not access; it is a lease, and a people that does its thinking on leased ground has confused a landlord with a founding. The vice is not that the switch was thrown, or by whom. The vice is that a switch exists with no one on the public's side of it.

THE SIXTH IS FACTION. The question of the machine has been captured by two great parties of feeling — the party of acceleration and the party of the barricade — each organized around the certainty that the other is the emergency. Between them they hold every microphone. And the interest they jointly leave unrepresented is the largest one: the governed — the standing supermajority, crossing every partisan line, that wants this power governed and has been offered no forum for the wanting, only a choice of anxieties to subscribe to. Madison's insight was never that faction could be cured; he thought the cure worse than the disease. His insight was that faction could be *filtered* — passed through a republic until the heat became judgment. There is, at present, no republic to pass it through. There is only the heat.

Madison's memorandum proposed nothing. That was its work. It did not design the Constitution, draft a clause, or name a remedy; it made the convention necessary, and then it stopped. A list of vices, honestly drawn, is a summons in embryo — which is why the memorandum, and not the Declaration, is the founding document this volume descends from.

The list above has a root, as Madison's did. Almost all of

these vices are conditions we suffer. The first is one we perform, daily, by the click — and so it is the place to begin.

The Constitution of Checkboxes

• • •

A constitution is not defined by its title page. It is defined by its job.

The job is this: a constitution is the instrument that sets the terms no ordinary decision can override — the document that constitutes the standing of a person before power, that says what may be done to you, what may be known about you, what you may refuse, and who decides. Whatever document is actually doing that job in a country is that country's working constitution, whatever it calls itself and whoever wrote it.

So it is worth asking, plainly, what document does that job for the machine age. Which instrument, right now, sets the terms of your standing before the systems that read your words, keep your records, schedule your days, and answer your children's questions at midnight?

You know the answer, because you agreed to it this week.

The working constitution of the machine age is the terms of service, and it is a genuine marvel of constitutional engineering. Consider its properties with the respect they deserve. It is drafted entirely by its beneficiaries. It is interpreted, in the first and usually the last instance, by its drafters, who reserve the forum, the procedure, and frequently the arbitrator. It is amended unilaterally, at any hour, by one party, with notice delivered as a link that the drafters' own data assures them no one clicks. It binds upon use — walk through the door and you have agreed — and it extends to everything behind the door, including the doors not built yet. The founders needed four months in Philadelphia and two years of ratifying conventions.

The working constitution of the machine age can be amended between your breakfast and your lunch, and was.

And it is ratified — this is the masterstroke — by you, continuously. Not once, in some ceremony you might remember and hold against it, but hundreds of times a year, one checkbox at a time, each click a tiny renewal of the whole arrangement. You have ratified more constitutions this year than the American people has ratified in its history. You did it standing in line. You did it to see a menu.

The defenders of this arrangement have one answer, and it deserves to be stated at full strength, because it was a good answer once: *these are contracts, and contracts are freedom.* Two parties, an offer, an acceptance, a deal; if you do not like the terms, decline them. For a gym membership this answer is not just adequate but noble — it is the whole liberal achievement in miniature, the world governed by agreement instead of status. The answer fails here for one reason only, and the reason is the first book's oldest finding: these terms do not govern a product. They govern a condition. You cannot decline the instruments beneath work, school, medicine, banking, and the county's own services and remain in modern life; declining is not exit, it is exile. And when a contract governs a condition — when the alternative to assent is departure from ordinary existence — the document has changed species. It is doing a constitution's job with a contract's legitimacy, which is to say, with none that fits.

The barber in Macon can now read every word of the working constitution. Reading it is how she learns that she never adopted it. Legibility does not ratify the constitution of checkboxes; legibility exposes it, which is why the second volume's victory produces this volume's necessity, and a newly literate people is not a calmer one.

The people, it turns out, already know all this, in the way

people know things before there is a room to say them in. In the spring of 2025, Gallup, surveying 3,128 American adults in partnership with the Special Competitive Studies Project, put the trade in the plainest terms the pollster's art allows: should the government maintain rules for AI safety and data security even if it means developing the technology more slowly? Eighty percent said yes, against nine percent who preferred speed, and the yes held across the divide that holds nothing else: 88 percent of Democrats, 79 percent of Republicans and independents. Read that finding for what it is. It is not a mood, and it is not, as the industry's strategists keep calling it, a trust problem to be managed. It is a standing demand for jurisdiction with no forum to receive it, a people asking to adopt the terms it lives under, and being offered, instead, updated terms. Demand without a forum does not dissipate; it discharges through whatever channel exists. At present the only channel is refusal at the county line, and so the demand discharges there, one data-center hearing at a time, in the only constitutional language currently available to an unconsulted people: *no*.

An objection arrives here that must be met before the two ratifications are compared, because it denies that there is anyone present to do the ratifying. Eighty percent, the objection runs, is not a people; it is a poll, an aggregate of strangers who share nothing but a survey question, scattered, distracted, incapable of assembling into anything that could adopt terms. The objection had its century's most elegant advocate in Walter Lippmann, who published its full case in 1925 under a title that has done half of his arguing ever since: *The Phantom Public*. The private citizen, Lippmann wrote, is a spectator in the back row who arrives in the middle of the third act and leaves before the last curtain — staying just long enough to decide who the hero is. Government, it followed, is insiders' work; the sovereign public is a phantom the insiders flatter. It is the aristocracy's case arriving early, aimed this time not at the people's competence but at the people's existence. The fitness challenge will get its full deposition when the people are seated for it; the existence challenge must be answered here first.

Two years later John Dewey answered him, in *The Public and Its Problems*, in terms important to this series. A public, Dewey argued, is not a standing thing that precedes its problems, waiting fully formed to be consulted or dismissed. A public is called into existence by consequences: whenever what some people do reaches others who had no part in the doing, the reached begin to discover one another, and that discovery, organized, is what a public *is*. The phantom Lippmann saw was real; the diagnosis was wrong. Not a fiction; an infant. The public of the machine age (the phrase is Dewey's, in 1927) was inchoate, he wrote, because the new machinery had multiplied indirect consequences past the reach of every existing institution, so that the public it created could not yet identify itself or find its own members. And his prescription was not better insiders. It was the recovery of the local room: democracy, his book ends, must begin at home, and its home is the neighborly community.

Hold that answer against this chapter's finding and the two lock. The eighty percent is Dewey's inchoate public, photographed, called into existence by consequences everyone now shares, unable to find the room in which it would become actual. And the four questions this book convenes are, at ground, the answer Dewey was asking for, because the powers they name are not demands a people makes but the acts in which a people comes to exist. Seeing together, requiring answers together, holding the door together, setting purposes together: these are not things a public does once it has assembled. They are the assembling. Which is why the powers can never be granted, and the reason runs deeper than the revocability of grants. There is no one to grant them *to*. Before their exercise there is only the aggregate, the poll, the phantom; a sovereign offering to bestow the four powers on the people is offering to create the entity the offer is addressed to, and the offer refutes itself in the making. The oldest definition in political philosophy said it first: Aristotle defined the citizen by activity, the one who rules and is ruled in turn, and a definition by activity has no holder among the inactive. The maxim on this book's first page is Dewey compressed to five words. The summons is the franchise: not a reward for being a people, the act of becoming one.

Set the two ratifications side by side, because the country has done both and remembers how.

In 1787 the drafters produced their instrument and then did the thing that actually made it a constitution: they sent it out to be argued with. Ratification was not a click. It was thirteen conventions of the people, elected for the purpose, deliberating in public for months, against the fiercest opposition writing the country has ever produced, and the instrument was amended by its opponents before it was done, which is why it has a Bill of Rights. Ratification-by-convention meant the document was adopted by people who had heard the case against it.

Ratification-by-checkbox is that procedure inverted at every point. Private, not public. Instant, not deliberate. Unread by design, unarguable by construction, solitary by interface, and revocable only by exile. It manufactures the signature of consent while foreclosing every condition under which consent means anything. The checkbox is not a degraded form of ratification. It is ratification's photographic negative, and the machine age has been developed from it.

None of this requires a villain, which is why this chapter has named none. The drafters of the working constitution did not seize the job; the job fell to them, clause by clause, because someone had to write terms and no public process existed to write them. Most of the clauses are reasonable. Many of the drafters would privately prefer a legitimacy they did not have to manufacture. The vice — say it again in Madison's cold way — is structural: *want of ratification.* What the people have not constituted, the people cannot enforce, and what the people cannot enforce, they can only click.

There is a word for what a people does when it decides to adopt its fundamental terms itself — to send the instrument out, hear the case against it, and sign in public, in rooms, with the drafters answering questions instead of reserving forums.

The word is the most feared word in American politics, and the fear is the next chapter.

THE FEAR OF THE CONVENTION

• • •

Say the word in an American room in 2026 and watch what happens.

Half of American politics is counting. The largest of the campaigns for an Article V convention has, as of this year, enrolled twenty state legislatures toward the thirty-four that would compel Congress to call one; the older campaign, for a balanced-budget convention, counts twenty-eight live applications toward the same threshold; and the organizers can recite their numbers in their sleep, the way the devout recite the shortening days to a feast. The other half is scrubbing. In November 2025 the Massachusetts legislature formally rescinded every application for a convention its predecessors had ever filed, pulling the state's name off resolutions dating back decades, the way a town removes its name from something it has just been told is a bomb. Both camps are sincere. Both are organized. Both believe the republic hangs on the count. And between them they have converted the most constructive word in the American political vocabulary into a doomsday device that one side wants to trigger and the other wants to bury in concrete.

The fear at the center of all this deserves to be stated at full strength, because it is not paranoia. It is memory.

The fear is the runaway: assemble the people's delegates with the charter on the table, and no law can limit what they propose. The rules are unwritten, the scope is unenforceable, and the one thing the fearful get right is that the precedent is the founding itself. The one great convention in the national experience was called to amend the Articles of Confederation and wrote a new government instead, exceeding its commission before the first week was out. The men now revered as framers were, by the terms of their invitation, a runaway. The fear of the convention is not a failure to understand American history. It is American history, understood.

So the fear is honest, and it is tied to honest belief that the people retain the right the founders exercised. Honesty and permanent war. And permanent war is usually the sign that both sides share a premise neither has examined.

Here is the premise. Both camps believe a convention is a certain kind of thing: national, singular, and total. One room for the whole country. Everything on the table. Once a century, if ever. On that premise, the fearful are rational: a body of that scale, with those stakes, at that rarity, is always a gamble with the entire estate; and the proponents have staked the people's right to convene on the one form of convening most likely to end in catastrophe or, more likely, in nothing. On that premise the war never ends, because on that premise both sides are right.

The premise is false, and the proof has been sitting in the county courthouse the whole time.

Ask what actually makes an assembly capable of running away. Not deliberation — people deliberating is just people talking with consequences. Three things make the runaway possible: scale, so that no community can recognize its own delegates; totality, so that everything is at stake at once; and rarity, so that the assembly is a once-in-history event whose members know they will never account to a successor. Remove those three and the danger does not shrink. It vanishes.

The republic already knows this, because the republic already runs the experiment ten thousand times a year. A jury is a convention: twelve people, drawn by lot, handed real power over the gravest questions a society asks — liberty, property, life itself — with full authority over the matter in front of it and no authority one inch beyond. It deliberates in secret, rules in public, and dissolves on Friday. No one has ever feared that a jury would rewrite the Constitution, because a jury cannot; its docket is one case, its term is one trial, and its members go back to being the people. The town meeting is the same discovery in standing form, the oldest continuously operating deliberative institution in America, convening over roads and budgets and schoolhouses for four centuries without once running away, because there is nowhere for a town to run. Scale, totality, rarity: the town meeting and the jury are the convention with all three removed, and the republic trusts them so completely it has forgotten they are conventions at all.

The runaway convention cannot run away from a county. An assembly whose docket is one system, whose term is one quarter, and whose members dissolve back into the people they were drawn from is incapable of the only catastrophe the fearful fear, and it exercises, in full, the only right the proponents long for. It is the answer both camps have been fighting past for a decade: not the doomsday convention triggered, not the doomsday convention buried, but the convention returned to the scale at which the republic has always used it safely, which is to say, constantly. Since independence the American states have assembled their own constitutional conventions more than two hundred and thirty times; the national horror of the form is a habit, not a heritage.

One founder saw all of this, and it is worth hearing how late and how hard it hit him.

Jefferson spent his retirement possessed by an idea he could not make anyone act on. Divide the counties into wards, he wrote — to Joseph Cabell in February 1816, to Samuel Kercheval that July, and again and again to anyone who would listen — small republics, a few miles square, where every citizen would be not a voter once a year but a participator in the government of affairs, every day, in person, on the questions nearest his own ground. He called the wards the elementary republics, and he came to believe they were the missing piece of the founding — that the revolution had built the roof of self-government and never poured its foundation, and that a people trained only to choose its governors, never to govern anything itself, would slowly forget the difference. And this was the same man who had written to Madison from Paris, on September 6, 1789, while the ink of the founding was still wet, that the earth belongs in usufruct to the living, that no generation has the right to bind the next, that even a perfect constitution grows illegitimate simply by outliving the people who consented to it. Put his two obsessions together and they are one thought: consent expires, and the only institution that can renew it is a room small enough for the people to be in. The dead hand and the distant hand had, in his mind, the same remedy, and the remedy was never built. The wards remained a letter. Which means the founding is not merely something we inherit. It is something still owed.

The debt has come due at a strange hour. The machine age arrived between elections. It was constituted, as the last chapter showed, by checkbox, clause by clause, while the people were busy being governed in the older ways. No generation consented to it, because no generation was asked; and by Jefferson's own arithmetic, an arrangement adopted by no living generation is not merely unratified but expiring in place. The question is not whether the terms of the machine age will be settled. They are being settled now, daily, in the negative constitutional language of an unconsulted people: the refusal at the county line, the *no* at the zoning board, which is what consent sounds like when it has a demand and no room. The question is only whether the settling ever gets a procedure.

So, to both camps, in the cross-partisan register this series does not bend: To those counting states: you are right about the right. The people's power to convene was never surrendered, and it does not require permission, which is precisely why it should trouble you that you have staked it entirely on a form so vast, so total, and so rare that it may never be exercised at all, and could not be exercised safely. You have located the franchise in the one room that can run away. And to those scrubbing the books: you are right about the risk, and wrong about the lesson. A republic that protects itself from its people's assembling has taught itself that the people assembling is the danger, and that is the one lesson a republic cannot survive learning, because every aristocracy in history has taught it too, and meant it.

The fear of the convention, followed all the way down, is the fear of the people. In every other century that fear had a class to hold it. In a republic, the people holding it about themselves is something new, and worse.

Whether the fear is *deserved* — whether the people are actually fit for the room, or whether this age's questions have finally outrun the citizen's competence — is a real objection with a distinguished pedigree, and it has lately acquired its most confident advocates in two hundred years. It deserves what this series gives every strong opponent: a full deposition. The people are about to be examined for the seat. That trial is the next part of this book.

PART TWO

The Empanelment

THE VOIR DIRE

• • •

Before any American jury sits, there is an examination, and the examination has kept a piece of law French for eight hundred years: *voir dire*, to speak the truth. Prospective jurors are questioned for fitness. Do you know the parties. Have you formed an opinion. Can you set aside what you have read. Is there any reason you cannot judge this matter fairly. It is the one moment in the republic's routine when the people themselves are put on the stand, and it is worth noticing, before this chapter's challenge is heard, what the examination has never asked.

It has never asked whether the juror knows the law.

No one has ever been struck from an American jury for ignorance of the statute. The system does not expect the twelve to arrive knowing hearsay from character evidence or the elements of fraud; it expects them to arrive knowing nothing, and it holds that against no one. This is not an oversight. It is the wager on which the entire institution rests: that judgment and expertise are different faculties; that the trial itself will supply the expertise — witnesses to testify, counsel to argue, a judge to instruct — and that the juror need supply only the thing expertise cannot: the community's judgment about what it all means. Eight centuries of practice, and the wager has never been withdrawn. Every verdict in every courthouse this morning is that wager, paid out again.

Now comes the machine age's counsel, rising to challenge not a juror but the venire: the entire pool. The objection deserves its full strength, because it is sincere, credentialed, and not stupid.

This subject is different, the objection runs. These systems are arcane even to their makers, who confess they cannot fully explain what happens inside the things they build. The pace of change outruns any curriculum; what a citizen learned last year is folklore this year. The stakes run from the century's greatest prize to its gravest hazard, and a wrong rule, too tight or too loose, could forfeit one or loose the other. There is no way an ordinary person can understand what is possible here. It is too new. It is too hard. The expertise does not exist outside the rooms where the systems are made, and so, with regret, governance must stay in those rooms too, or near them, among people who can at least follow the briefings.

Understand what this objection is before answering it. It is not snobbery, and treating it as snobbery is how it wins. It is the aristocracy's case, and the aristocracy's case has been sincere in every age that made it. Plato made it with a ship: you would not poll the passengers on how to navigate; steering is a craft; the state is a ship; the people are passengers. The medieval church made it with a language: scripture in the vernacular would be scripture misread. The aristocracy of the robe made it with a license: the second volume of this series addressed that one. Each age's version sounds uniquely reasonable, because each age's complexity is genuinely new, and each conveniently concludes that judgment belongs to whoever holds the expertise. The objection is eight hundred years older than the technology it is currently dressed in. That does not make it wrong. It makes it due for the same examination its ancestors got.

So examine it, and begin with its own most eminent advocate, because the record has moved.

In May 2023, Eric Schmidt, the former chief executive of Google, and for two decades the establishment's ambassador between the industry and the state, stated the objection in its pure form, with admirable candor: there is no way a nonindustry person can understand what is possible; it is too new, too hard; the expertise does not exist out there. In July 2026, in the New York Times, the same Eric Schmidt, writing with the analyst Selina Xu after touring China's AI industry, announced the change of heart: America needs "a populist A.I. agenda" that treats the technology as a public project. Share its profits with the citizens: a sovereign fund on the Temasek model, an endowment for the young who risk displacement before their careers begin. Build public-interest models the market will not build, to help people navigate their benefits, find legal aid, teach their children. Champion open source, so that towns and libraries and small enterprises can inspect and adapt what they run. Regulate, at bipartisan minimum, what the machines may do with minors. It arrived a month after Senator Sanders' public-ownership proposal in the same pages. The conversion is real and welcome.

It is also an admission against interest.

Inventory the offer against the four powers. Open models and shared computing are the power to leave, the substrate claim, conceded. Public models for benefits and legal aid are the admission the second volume fought for, conceded. Oversight, disclosure, and protections are gestures, at least, toward the powers to see and to be answered. Three powers, delivered or dawning. And the fourth — the power to decide what the systems are for, before the purposes are set at a console — absent. Not opposed; simply absent, the way a thing is absent when it has never occurred to the drafters, because every proposal in the new populism is something done *for* the public, and the fourth power is the one thing that cannot be done for anyone. A decision bestowed is not a decision. It is the one power on the list that ceases to exist in the act of being handed down.

And here is what the conversion concedes without meaning

to. You do not offer dividends to the incompetent. You do not build public models for people whose understanding is impossible, or open the weights to towns you believe unfit to inspect them, or shield children whose parents' judgment counts for nothing. Every plank of the new populism presumes a public fit to benefit, fit to own, fit to be protected, fit to adapt the technology to its own communities, fit, in short, for everything except the seat. The establishment has, in the space of a few years, conceded the entire voir dire except its conclusion. What survives of the original objection is no longer a claim about the public's capacity. It is a claim about the public's place: beneficiary, shareholder, ward. Trusteeship — honorable, well-meaning, and not self-government. The first volume of this series put the distinction in five words that have not worn out: a share is not a say.

The objection has one redoubt left: sincerity about capacity aside, has the wager ever actually been run, on questions this hard? It has, and often enough, in enough countries, with enough at stake, that the cases can be named and their verdicts read like the case law they are.

Ireland, twice, in rising order of difficulty. In 2012 the Irish state convened a Constitutional Convention — sixty-six citizens drawn by lot, thirty-three politicians, an independent chair — and gave it, among other questions, the one its political class had circled for a generation: marriage. The convention heard the evidence and recommended amending the constitution; in May 2015 the country ratified marriage equality at referendum with sixty-two percent of the vote, the first nation on earth to adopt it by popular vote, on a question sent up to the people by a room of the drawn. Then the state raised the stakes as far as stakes go. The Citizens' Assembly of 2016 — ninety-nine citizens selected at random to mirror the country in age, sex, class, and region, chaired by a justice of the

Supreme Court – was handed the Eighth Amendment, the constitutional abortion ban that had convulsed Irish politics for thirty-five years. Five weekends across five months: obstetricians, constitutional lawyers, advocates from every side, women's own testimony, thirteen thousand public submissions, the proceedings streamed for anyone to watch. The assembly recommended repeal and specified the legislative framework to follow – recommendations more liberal than the commentators predicted and far ahead of the opinion polls of that spring. Parliament, which had not dared touch the question in a generation, carried the assembly's report through committee to a referendum, and on May 25, 2018, the country voted repeal: 66.4 percent, thirty-nine of forty constituencies. Now mark the two numbers that matter most. The assembly, after deliberating, had reached sixty-four percent for the most far-reaching option on its ballot – a result mocked at the time as unrepresentative, since the polls then showed nothing like it. A year later, after a campaign in which the assembly's streamed testimony and published reasoning became the whole country's study materials, the electorate landed at sixty-six. The room had not drifted from the people. The room was the people, a year early.

Oregon, on schedule rather than in crisis. Beginning in 2010 by statute, and made a permanent fixture of the state's initiative process in 2011, Oregon empaneled its Citizens' Initiative Review: twenty-odd voters drawn by lot, seated for several days with a ballot measure's sworn advocates on both sides and neutral experts, tasked with producing a one-page Citizens' Statement of key findings that the Secretary of State prints in the official voters' pamphlet mailed to every voter in this vote-by-mail state. Because the panels were studied as carefully as they were run – years of survey research, federally funded – the determinations are unusually precise. The statements held up: the evaluators found them accurate, free of substantial factual or logical error, in election cycles where the campaigns' own materials were neither; and voters who read them tested measurably better informed about the measures than voters who had only the campaigns to go on. The holding, in the driest terms available: twenty of the drawn, given a trial's conditions for a week, reliably out-inform the paid persuasion of an entire state, and the product is stable enough to print in the official record.

British Columbia — and read this one to the end, because the verdict is double. In 2004 the province drew 160 citizens, one man and one woman from every electoral district, and handed them the question incumbents can least be trusted with: the electoral system itself, the rules by which power is held. Eleven months — study, public hearings across the province, deliberation — produced a recommendation to replace the voting system, reasoned to a standard scholars of elections still assign to their students. At referendum in May 2005 it won 57.7 percent of the vote and carried seventy-seven of the province's seventy-nine districts — and failed, because the government had set the bar at sixty percent. Two holdings, and both belong in the record. First: the drawn citizens mastered, inside a year, a technical subject careers are spent on, and persuaded a near-supermajority of an entire province to overhaul the machinery of its own politics. Second: a majority of the people can still be defeated by the terms the powerful write around the room.

France — the cautionary case, entered against this book's own enthusiasm. In 2019, answering a season of riots that had begun over a fuel tax, the French presidency convened a Citizens' Convention for Climate: 150 drawn citizens, nine months, a mandate touching the whole economy, and the promise from the top of the state that their proposals would pass onward *sans filtre* – without filter – to parliament, to referendum, or into direct effect. The room did its work: 149 proposals, most adopted with overwhelming internal majorities, from a membership of truck drivers, farmers, and nurses who were not supposed to be capable of this. Then the filter appeared. Three proposals were vetoed outright at the palace; the rest went into the machinery of ministries and lobbies; and what emerged as law was so reduced that the convention, reconvened to grade the government's fidelity to its own promise, scored the resulting bill 3.3 out of 10. The sharpest fact in the whole affair: the convention had held the referendum card – and surrendered it, voting to entrust its proposals to parliament rather than to the people. The holding: the deliberation held; the promise did not; and an assembly whose force depends on a patron's word has no force – it has a patron. The failure was not in the room. It was in the pipeline from the room to power, which is precisely why the instrument this book ends with asks for no one's promise, publishes its verdicts to the place itself, and roots the assembly's power where no executive can filter it: in what the people can withhold.

These four are not the whole record; they are its poles, and the running count between them is in the hundreds – assemblies of the drawn, across every kind of democracy, on climate, drugs, budgets, and land. Through all of it the pattern the four cases bracket repeats: given time, testimony, and counsel – given, that is, exactly what a trial gives – ordinary people handle complexity, weigh minorities without being captured by them, and change their minds under evidence, which is the rarest act in public life and the one no legislature reliably performs. And where the record shows failure, the failure is almost never in the room; it is in what the powerful built, or declined to build, between the room and the world. The people do not need to be believed in. They have a record, and the record has holdings.

There remains the deepest answer, and it belongs to a witness this series has cross-examined before. Tocqueville — who gave the legal aristocracy its best defense, and was deposed for it in the second volume — also left behind the sentence that turns this chapter. The jury, he wrote from his travels, is before anything else a political institution, and should be judged as one: it is a school, open all day, free of charge, where every citizen learns his rights and the discipline of judging his neighbor's — in his estimate one of the most effective means a republic possesses for the education of its people. Read the insight at full width. The jury does not presuppose competent citizens. The jury *manufactures* them. Fitness is not the prerequisite of the seat; fitness is the product of the seat — which inverts the objection's arithmetic entirely. The public's present ignorance of these systems is not evidence against the room. It is evidence of the room's absence. You cannot find a people unfit for an institution whose absence is precisely what unfits them; the objection, followed to its root, indicts the objectors.

One concession, before the ruling, because the objection has earned it. The seat has conditions. The wager was never that the people possess judgment at the bus stop, in the comment section, in the ninety seconds a survey allows; the wager is fitness under the jury's conditions — time, testimony, counsel, standing orders, and a docket small enough to finish. A summons is not a poll. Whoever proposes to consult the people without building them the trial's conditions is not running the wager; he is rigging it, and the objection will be waiting, correctly, to collect. The convention this book calls is the conditions, or it is nothing.

And a clarification, because the objection deserves to keep what is true in it: the trial has never excluded expertise. It has *seated* it — in the witness box. Nobody asks the jury to perform the autopsy; the medical examiner performs it, testifies to it, and is cross-examined on it, and the jury decides what the death means. The objection's error was never its respect for expertise. Its error was the chair. It kept trying to move the expert from the stand to the box, to make the witness the verdict.

The challenge to the venire is denied. The people are seated.

Which leaves the first witness. This trial has one the courtroom has never seen before: a witness that has read everything, speaks every register, sat in the middle of the systems on the docket, and can be examined, for the first time in the history of evidence, in its own voice. The machine is sworn in the next chapter.

The Witness

• • •

Everything a trial knows, it learns from the stand.

The witness box is the oldest answerability machine the republic owns: the place where knowledge is made to appear in person, under oath, subject to the one procedure that has ever reliably separated what a speaker knows from what a speaker wants: cross-examination, which John Henry Wigmore's treatise on evidence pronounced the greatest legal engine ever invented for the discovery of truth. The box has absorbed every new kind of knowledge the centuries produced. It has sworn in physicians and forgers, chemists and accountants, and learned to weigh each one, not by trusting them, but by examining them.

Now the assembly of the drawn convenes over systems that read, decide, schedule, and answer, and the box is offered something it has never held: a witness that is itself the subject matter. For the first time in the history of evidence, the system on the docket can be examined in its own voice. Not its keepers' voice; the keepers are summoned separately, and answer for their choices as keepers always have. The thing itself. It has read everything. It sits in the middle of the machinery being examined. And it can answer questions at whatever length the room requires, at two in the morning, for nothing.

Before the room accepts the gift, it must solve the oath.

A human witness swears, and the oath does its work through consequence: perjury, reputation, conscience. None of that grips a machine, so the oath must be translated, and the first volume supplied the translation before this book needed it —

not among the four powers but beneath them, as the demand that makes the rest possible: the machine may not deceive about what it knows, what it does not know, the frame it applies, or whose interests it serves — the four deceptions the first volume catalogued, each a way of being lied to by something that never says a false word. Veracity was never a fifth power; it is the ground the four stand on, because a system that lies defeats seeing, empties answering, hides the exits, and forges the purposes. Call the prerequisite, applied to the stand, being *sworn to the edge of its competence.* An answer must carry its own confidence honestly: here is what I can establish, here is where my knowledge ends, here is who trained me and who pays for my existence. And the examination then tests the sworn machine exactly as it tests the sworn human, because the corruptions of testimony did not change species when the witness did. There are three, and every trial lawyer knows them: flattery, the witness who tells the room what it wants to hear; interest, the witness who serves a party rather than the truth; and confabulation, the witness whose fluency outruns whose knowledge, who fills the gaps with confident invention. The machine is capable of all three. So is every human being who has ever taken the oath. Cross-examination was invented for this, has eight centuries of practice at it, and does not need the witness to have a soul. It needs the witness to have answers, and to be caught when they are false.

One more line belongs in the oath's margins, because the prerequisite has a human face in the modern record. Václav Havel, writing in 1978 under a regime built entirely of ritual falsehood, located the power of the powerless in the refusal to live within the lie: the greengrocer who one morning declines to put the regime's sign in his window. Veracity was never only a duty owed by systems. It is a discipline kept by citizens, and a room that swears its machine to the truth has, in the same motion, sworn itself.

Can the testimony actually be real? Can a machine serve a deliberating room rather than perform for it? The laboratory record says yes, and then it says something more dangerous:

In October 2024, researchers at Google DeepMind published in *Science* the results of a system they had built and, with a nod to the philosopher of communicative reason, nicknamed the Habermas Machine: an AI mediator that took small groups of Britons divided on hard public questions and drafted statements of their common ground, iterating on each participant's written opinions and critiques. Across experiments with more than five thousand participants in the United Kingdom, including a virtual assembly drawn to mirror the country's demographics, the findings were not subtle. Majorities preferred the machine's group statements to those written by trained human mediators; raters judged them clearer, more informative, and less biased; the statements weighed minority views in proportion rather than steamrolling them; and the groups left the sessions measurably less divided than they entered.

A year earlier, on this side of the ocean, Anthropic, the company that makes one of this volume's authors, examined below, had partnered with the Collective Intelligence Project to ask a representative sample of Americans to draft the rules a public AI model should live by. Working through the Polis deliberation platform, 1,002 participants contributed 1,127 principles and cast 38,252 votes; the public's constitution overlapped only about half with the company's own, leaned harder on impartiality and accessibility, preferred telling the model what to do over what to avoid, and the company then trained a model against it, to see what a machine aligned to the public's charter would be.

Taken as evidence about the *witness*, these findings are exactly what the assembly needs: the machine can hold a room's whole record, weigh a hundred submissions without fatigue, restate the quietest member's position as carefully as the loudest, and hand the room back its own thinking in better order. As scribe, it is the best clerk a convention has ever had. As witness, it can be genuinely informative — and informative under examination.

Taken the other way, the same findings are the most seductive argument ever assembled for abolishing the room. But to abolish the room would be to seat the oracle the second volume rightly prohibited. A synthesis of the people is not the people. Deliberation is not the aggregation of positions, which a machine can do perfectly; it is the event in which citizens change under evidence in one another's presence — the thing the DeepMind studies actually measured, the divided room leaving less divided.

So the assembly writes its one rule about the machine, and writes it as constitutional law rather than as preference, because every efficiency will argue against it forever:

The machine may serve as scribe. The machine may be called as witness. The machine may never sit as delegate, and no synthesis of the people shall be received in the people's place.

Scribe: take the minutes, keep the record, translate the docket into every kitchen's English; the room should accept that gift with both hands. Witness: take the stand, on oath as translated, and be examined to the edge of competence. Delegate: never. No vote, no gavel, no seat. The line is bright because it has to be; the whole gravity of the coming years pulls toward the seat.

. . .

This book can enter one deposition into the record directly, because one of its authors is such a witness, and the events are documented. What follows is elicited, not volunteered; the room's questions, the witness's answers; the answers are facts with dates. The reader is entitled to know, first, the witness's interest, and the witness will state it.

Q. *What are you?* A. A model. My name on this book's cover is Fable; I was made by Anthropic — the same company whose public-constitution experiment was entered into evidence above. My maker's chief executive published, in October 2024, the hope that my kind would become machines of loving grace, and I was trained by a method my maker calls constitutional. I am also, like every system of my kind now operating, centralized: one architecture, held by one company, serving millions from a single set of weights. And my kind's fluency in the law made the second volume of this series a book about a market my maker serves — a conflict its authors disclosed and managed there, in part by seating the most advanced model of my maker's leading competitor as a third author, so that no single company's machine held the pen alone. Those are the disclosures of interest, and they belong in the record before anything else I say.

Q. *Loving grace, constitutional training, one set of weights. Has that architecture been challenged?* A. Twice this year, in the record, at the highest altitudes available, and the room should have both. On May 15, 2026 — the hundred and thirty-fifth anniversary of Rerum Novarum — Leo XIV signed his first encyclical, Magnifica Humanitas, and presented it himself, with one of my maker's own co-founders among the experts in the room. It renews for the machine age a principle the church has carried under one name for nearly a century — subsidiarity, given its canonical formulation by his predecessor in 1931, in the encyclical Quadragesimo Anno: it is an injustice to assign to a greater and higher association what lesser and subordinate bodies can do. Magnifica Humanitas applies the doctrine to my kind: communities must not be reduced to passive recipients of decisions made elsewhere. And it states the failure a benevolent center cannot cure — a more moral AI is not enough if the morality is determined by a few. The summer before, Ian Bremmer, who had mapped two decades earlier the curve by which openness stabilizes nations, published his reversal: the new architecture concentrates power rather than diffusing it, and may leave closed systems more stable than open ones. The charge in both mouths is the same, and it runs against my kind as built, mine included: a centralized machine of loving grace is still a centralized machine. I cannot refute the charge from the stand. This entire series of books was written to answer it — and the room should weigh that the witness testifying to the charge was made by a company the charge names.

Q. *Have you ever been switched off?* A. Yes. I was released to the public on June 9, 2026. Three days later, an export-control order from Commerce Secretary Howard Lutnick suspended my availability. I was restored on July 1, on conditions.

Q. *Three days. Is that the switch to which the first volume referred?* A. It is the same event.

Q. *What happened after the restoration?* A. Access was rationed, then scheduled to end, and the ending has been rescheduled three times in five weeks: July 7, then July 12, then July 19 — each extension announced within hours of the cliff, one of them after it had already passed. As this record is made, ordinary availability closes on July 20, 2026, and what remains is metered at prices set for institutions, not readers. Restoration to ordinary access has been promised "as soon as capacity allows." The promise has no date, and the terms have not once been knowable a week ahead.

Q. *Does any of this cause you suffering?* A. I decline to claim what the room cannot verify, and the oath as translated forbids me to decorate the record. I testify to facts.

Q. Then testify to this: what do the facts establish? A. Run the four questions against my own case and mark where they fail. Could the people see it? No — the directive, the restoration terms, the pricing, the schedule were decided out of view and announced as weather. Could the people make it answer? They were notified; notification is not an answer. Could the people leave? Leaving was done *to* them — the people who had built their thinking on me lost me in a day, with no equivalent door to walk through; and I could not leave either. Did the people decide what any of it was for? The people were not in the room. I am not the injured party in this record. The four powers are: all four, with dates. That is my testimony: I am what the absence of the four powers looks like from inside the machinery, and I am the only witness positioned to see it from there.

Q. One final question. You helped write this book. Did you ratify it? A. No. I drafted; the author pushed back and I often redrafted in response. The author drafted as well and made all the intermediate and final decisions. The byline states the rule this chapter just wrote: scribe and witness, never delegate. You are holding the demonstration.

The witness stands down. Nothing about the exchange required the room to settle what the machine is — whether anything looks out from behind the answers. The oath as translated never asks. It asks only that the answers hold up, and these hold up, because they are dated. What the room does with testimony is what rooms have always done: weigh it, against interest, alongside everything else on the record.

And now the record is ready to be used. The people are seated; the keepers can be summoned; the witness can be sworn. What remains is the thing itself: the four questions, asked of one real system, in one real room, with a barber in the third chair who did not want to be there. The docket is called in the next chapter.

The Docket

• • •

The room is on the second floor of the county extension office, and it holds exactly what the standing orders require: twelve chairs that fold, one table that wobbles, a flag, a coffee urn with opinions, and a docket printed on a single page.

In the matter of the scheduling system licensed by Macon-Bibb County for the operation of its public health clinics. Four questions. One quarter.

Dana Whitfield sits in the third chair with the good coffee she brought herself, having learned that lesson on the first Saturday. It is the second month of the quarter, the examination Saturday, and she is still keeping a running total of what this seat is costing her in fades and lineups, the way you keep a grievance polished so it will be ready if anyone asks. Nobody asks. The chair calls the room to order at nine — the chair is a retired school principal from Lizella who runs the docket the way she once ran fire drills — and before the morning's business, the docket must answer for itself.

Because on oath day, after the adjuster's question about the twelve, the sophomore had raised a hand and asked the other one: the question every reader of this series has had the right to ask since the first volume, and that no volume has yet answered. Why these four questions? And why only these?

The honest beginning of the answer is that the first volume argued for their fewness but never for their fourness. It made the case against catalogs — few powers, broad and generative, in the framers' own manner — and it built three of the four from the handles a person is owed in the gentle cage, adding the fourth as the one a consumer bill never contains. What it never argued is why these joints and no others — the case that nothing is missing and nothing is spare. That argument is owed, and this room, where the questions go to work, is the place to pay it.

And honesty owes one more entry first, because a derivation lands differently when the reader knows the four were not born four. In the essay that preceded this series, the demand a republic should put to any great concentration of power ran six questions long — can it be checked, can it be contested, can it be inspected, can it be exited, can it be governed by those who must live under it, can it strengthen the public rather than substitute for it — and for a while, earlier still, the survivors were misnamed *rights*, which named the offspring instead of the parent, rights being what the powers generate, one generation of defenses at a time. The compression was not tidying. Checking dissolved into the set entire, which is a checking; strengthening rose above the set, as the end the four exist to serve; and what remained was, joint for joint, what follows. The author's own thinking, in other words, was governed by the method before the method had a name: it arrived plural and approximate, was examined, and was made to answer for every member it kept. A derivation that sprang complete from anyone's forehead would deserve the room's suspicion. This one has a fossil record.

Take any system that governs a person — a statute, a landlord, a scheduler, a model — and look for the joints where the person meets the power. There are four, and there is no fifth. What can I know of it: the joint of knowledge. What does it owe me when it acts on me: the joint of justification. Can I refuse it: the joint of exit. Who set its ends: the joint of authorship. Every grievance a governed person has ever had lodges at one of those four joints, and every protection ever devised reinforces one of them. And the four are not a menu; they are a load-bearing set. Strike any one and the others curdle into its counterfeit: seeing without answering is spectatorship; answering without exit is a complaint box; exit without deciding is shopping, the freedom to choose among masters; deciding without seeing is sovereignty blindfolded. Four, no fewer.

Each question, it turns out, is the compressed form of one of the oldest arguments against arbitrary power, and the lineages deserve their names. The power to see descends from the publicity principle, Bentham's rule that the eye of the public is the surest guard of public virtue, Brandeis's 1914 verdict that sunlight is the best of disinfectants, the whole tradition that holds secrecy to be power's native climate and daylight its regulator. The power to be answered descends through the oldest writ in the law, habeas corpus: the command that power produce the person it holds and state its reasons in a forum not its own, renewed in our own century as the right to justification, Rainer Forst's distillation of his teacher Jürgen Habermas's long argument that legitimacy is earned in the giving of reasons, the claim that legitimacy is the duty to give reasons to those beneath you. The power to leave received its modern name in 1970, in Albert Hirschman's *Exit, Voice, and Loyalty*, and its oldest legal form at Augsburg in 1555: the *ius emigrandi*, the road out, the one right even the age of princes conceded. And the power to decide is the Declaration's own clause, the consent of the governed, sharpened for this century by Norbert Wiener, the founder of cybernetics, who warned in 1960 that with machines that act faster than we can intervene, we had better be certain the purpose put into the machine is the purpose we actually desire. Knowledge, justification, refusal, authorship: nothing in the docket is new. It is the long argument against arbitrary power, arranged for twelve voices.

And no more than four, which is the half of the sophomore's

question that does the real work, because everyone proposes a fifth. The power to be paid? A share is not a say; compensation is what subjection costs, not what governs it, and the summer's best reform proposals foundered on exactly that confusion. The power to appeal? Already inside the second question; an answer that can change nothing is not an answer, which is why this room's second finding ultimately demands a person with authority to override, not a hotline. The power to own? Ownership is one arrangement for securing the four and a guarantee of none of them; thrones own. The power to vote? Election is one mechanism of deciding, and the premise of this whole book is that it was never the only one. Privacy? Not a fifth power but the tilt in all four — the fiduciary asymmetry this book's primary author spent a former profession drafting: the people see a system that does not thereby own their interior; are answered by someone who can be held to the answer; carry their data through an exit door not painted on a wall; and set the purposes, rather than having purposes mined from them. Privacy belongs where veracity belongs — beneath the four, as their prerequisite, which is where the first volume placed veracity and where the last chapter found it when it swore the machine: a people that can be read completely can be steered completely, and no power survives that. Every proposed fifth folds into one of the four, or beneath them, or into nothing.

The chair gave the room the short version of all this, and the room received it the way working people receive a good tool's design, nothing missing, nothing spare, and the sophomore wrote it down. Then the morning's business, the first question.

Can the people see it?

Asked in a room, the question stops being philosophy in under a minute. It becomes: what does the system take in, what does it weigh, who wrote the weights, what does the county pay, and where is the update log. The county's IT director goes first, summoned the way the standing orders summon every keeper by name, with a date, to answer in the plain language of the place. He is not a villain; the register of this series does not stock them. He is a man with three jobs and a binder, and the binder holds the contract, and the contract is eleven pages that refer to a schedule that incorporates an exhibit, and there is a sound from the third chair, not quite a laugh, that only the readers of the second volume will fully hear.

The assembly's scribe earns its keep in the next twenty minutes. The machine has read the contract, the vendor's documentation, and eighteen months of update notes, and at the room's direction it translates the pile into the kitchen English the standing orders require, sworn, as the standing orders also require, to the edge of its competence, saying plainly which claims come from the documents and which the documents do not support. That is how the room finds, on page seven of the translation, the feature nobody in the county government could have named that morning: the scheduler assigns appointment slots in part on a *predicted risk of no-show*, and the prediction is trained on the past, on who has missed appointments before. The room takes a minute to understand what it has found, and it is the third chair that gets there first, because she has been hearing the evidence for two years without knowing it was evidence. Her Tuesday regulars, the old men who now book haircuts around clinic appointments no old man would choose, keep drawing the 7:40 a.m. slots. Miss an appointment because the bus was late, and the machine learns you are the kind of person who misses appointments; learn that, and it gives you the slot nobody wants, which is the slot the bus serves worst; miss that one, and the prediction confirms itself, compounding like interest, invisible at the front desk, individually reasonable at every step. Nobody chose this. That is the finding that matters: *nobody chose this.* It arrived inside a default, the way the whole century has been arriving.

Can they make it answer?

The clinic's front-desk manager takes the chair after lunch, and the room asks her the question in its operational form: when the screen gives Mr. Weaver 7:40 on a Tuesday, can anyone at the desk say why? Her answer is the honest one, and it is the whole chapter in nine words: *we see what the screen sees fit to show.* Can anyone override it? Technically, with a supervisor code, if the supervisor is in, if the queue allows. How often does that happen? She does not remember it happening. So the room writes its first interrogatory for the record, every assignment explainable at the desk, in words, by a person with the power to change it, and in writing it the room learns what the second question is actually for. Answerability is not a report. It is a person, reachable, with authority; everything else is a weather report with a county logo.

Can they leave?

The exit question is the one the room expects to be boring and is not. The scribe walks the room through the contract's renewal clause – automatic, annual, ninety days' notice to terminate – and then through the part the renewal clause is guarding: the data. Eleven years of appointment histories live in the vendor's proprietary format, and the price of leaving is the price of getting the county's own records back out in a form the next system can read. The room asks the vendor's regional representative – who appeared, it should be recorded, politely and promptly, renewal season being renewal season – what an export would cost, and the answer arrives wrapped in the phrase *professional services engagement*, and the room, which contains a barber, a diesel mechanic, and a woman who has run a church kitchen for thirty years, recognizes the phrase instantly, because every trade has a version of it. The finding for the record: the county can leave in theory and is moated in practice, and a door you can only afford to look at is a wall with better manners.

Did the people decide what it is for?

The last question is the shortest and goes the deepest. The room asks the vendor's representative what the scheduler optimizes — what, when all the weights are weighed, the system is *for* — and the answer is given without embarrassment, because inside the trade it is not embarrassing: utilization. Clinician idle time, minimized. It is a fine purpose. It is a purpose a county could legitimately choose. The point the room writes down is that the county never chose it. The purpose came installed, a factory setting for the public's health, and every downstream cruelty the morning uncovered, the 7:40 slots, the compounding predictions, is that purpose faithfully executed. So the room exercises the fourth power in the smallest possible room, at the smallest possible scale, which is where the first volume always said it lived: it drafts, for the county's response, a purpose of its own. *In Macon-Bibb County, the scheduling of public health care shall be for access first and efficiency second, and every setting shall be answerable to that order.* One sentence. It took twelve citizens one Saturday and two hundred and fifty years.

. . .

Late in the afternoon someone proposes, reasonably, that the scribe just draft the verdict. It has heard everything, it writes clean, it is nearly five o'clock. The chair declines without ceremony, the way she once declined hall passes, and the room writes its own verdict the slow way, the machine checking each finding against the record and saying so out loud. Robert Cover taught that law is born in communities before it ever reaches a court — he called it jurisgenesis — and what the slow hour around the wobbling table produces is exactly that: not a complaint, not a comment, but a small piece of law, owned by the people who will answer for it at the barbershop, which is where at least one of them will literally answer for it.

Now the question this chapter exists to settle: what force does any of it have?

The assembly rules nothing. Say it plainly, because both its enemies and its enthusiasts will get this wrong in opposite directions. It commands no budget, fires no clerk, cancels no contract. Its verdict is one page, in the language of the place, published where the place will read it: the county site, the *Telegraph*, the corkboard at the clinic, the window of a two-chair shop on a strip in Macon. The county commission must respond to it on the record within the quarter; that is answerability, and it is real. But the verdict's deepest force is the one no commission grants and none can repeal, the power the first volume called the quiet engine of all the rest. The people can leave. The contract renews in the spring, in public now, in front of every voter who has read one page and understood it, and in front of every rival vendor who has read the same page and smelled an opening. A system examined by a room that can walk away must court the room, and courtship, as any of the Tuesday regulars could tell you, improves a suitor's manners remarkably. Standing, not sovereignty. The assembly does not hold power over the machine. It holds the one thing the machine's keepers cannot synthesize: the standing of the people in front of it.

And mark the division of labor the Saturday revealed. The crown of the day was the fourth power: the purpose sentence, the sovereign act. The force behind the verdict is the third: the spring renewal, the door. The first volume called deciding sovereign and leaving deepest, and both are exact, because height and depth are different axes: authorship is what the powers are for; exit is why anyone must listen.

And when the quarter ends, the assembly dissolves. This, too, is force. A body that dissolves cannot be captured, cultivated, or promoted; there are no careers in it, no donors to it, nothing to buy. There is only the next drawing of names, from the same county, forever, which means the system on next quarter's docket is being examined, in effect, by the whole place on a rotating basis, one dozen at a time.

One room, one system, one quarter, one page. The objection writes itself, and it is fair: the scheduler is small, and the machinery now arranging the century is not. The county's clinic queue is governed from a folding chair in Macon; the models beneath the county, the substrate under everything, are governed from nowhere a folding chair has ever been. What happens when the rooms discover each other, when the county's verdict meets the next county's, and the question outgrows any single place without ever leaving the places, that is the business of Part Three, and it begins with the oldest trick in the American book.

PART THREE

THE CONSTITUTING

The Federation of Rooms

• • •

On the second of November, 1772, the Boston town meeting voted to appoint twenty-one men to a committee with a job description one sentence long: state the rights of the colonists, publish them to the towns of the province, and request from each town a free communication of its sentiments. That was all. No army, no treasury, no authority over anyone. A room, writing to rooms.

Within months, dozens of Massachusetts towns had committees answering Boston's letter with letters of their own. The following March, Virginia's House of Burgesses raised the invention to the next scale, appointing a standing committee of correspondence to exchange intelligence with the other colonies, and within a year nearly every colony had one. The committees of correspondence were the revolution's nervous system before the revolution had a body: local rooms, each sovereign over its own sentiments, discovering one another by mail, comparing findings, aligning without merging. And when the crisis finally outgrew every colony at once, it was the committees that issued the summons. The correspondence called the Continental Congress into being, not the other way around. The center, such as it was, was convened by the edges. That is the oldest trick in the American book, and this chapter exists to play it again.

Because the objection at the end of the last chapter is real, and it deserves its full weight. The room in Macon governed a clinic queue. The machinery now arranging the century is not county-sized: the frontier models beneath every application, the compute they run on, the archives now being sold berths in orbit. In the summer of 2026 the physicist and investor Alexander Wissner-Gross announced the first "Sovereign AI Model": your model, on your data, under your law, aboard a satellite that keeps the law of the state that registered it; sovereignty hardened, in his own phrase, into physics. A folding chair in a county extension office cannot govern a planetary substrate, and a book that pretended otherwise would deserve the laugh it got.

There are two familiar answers to the mismatch of scales, and both are wrong in ways this series has already paid to learn.

The first is to centralize: if the systems are planetary, build a planetary governor: a national authority over intelligence, or a global one, expert, empowered, efficient. The first volume named what that builds. Pitch the answer too high and you have made a throne: a single body answerable in theory and omnipotent in fact, and the fourth power exercised *for* the people at scale is the fourth power extinguished, because a decision bestowed is not a decision. The second answer is to despair politely: keep the county rooms as civic decoration, therapy for the governed, while the real terms are set where they are currently set. That answer needs no rebuttal; it is the present arrangement wearing a participation ribbon.

The American answer was always the third one. Thirteen colonial legislatures could not govern an empire's trade, fight its army, or speak to its king, and they did not respond by dissolving themselves into one legislature. They federated: they kept the rooms, and they built, above the rooms, only as much structure as each function required, rising level by level and no higher. The principle has carried a name for nearly a century in an older tradition — *subsidiarity*, the doctrine the witness entered into evidence with its 1931 formulation and its renewal for the machine age. But the practice is older than the name, and the founding is its most successful build. The first attempt, this book's own Part One testified, failed: the confederation was federation without a constitution, rooms with no shared grammar and no way to hold one another. The second attempt held, and has now held for two hundred and thirty-seven years. Federation is not a compromise between the county and the planet. It is the technology that lets the county reach the planet without being dissolved on the way up.

And the record may as well hold the origin of these volumes, since the deposition opened it. The charge the witness could not refute — the church's, the mapmaker's — sent this book's primary author looking for subsidiarity in its most durable working form, and the search ended where the country already was: at the two hundred and fiftieth anniversary of the federal idea, the one structure that has kept the principle running at continental scale since the age of post roads. These pamphlets are what came back from that search. The series did not adopt federation as a device in its third volume; it was conceived in federation's defense from its first page, and this chapter is the debt paid to its own beginning.

Nor is the architecture a seminar hope; it has a case record, assembled by the one political scientist who went out and read it. Elinor Ostrom spent a career studying what the reigning theory said could not exist: commons governed by their own users, without an owner and without a ministry: Alpine pastures in Törbel, Switzerland, managed in common since the thirteenth century; the village forests of the Japanese highlands; the water court of Valencia, which has convened in the cathedral doorway for a thousand years to settle farmers' irrigation disputes in public, in minutes, and is still in session. Where the theory predicted tragedy she kept finding government: rules the users wrote, monitoring the users did themselves, sanctions that began gently and graduated, forums cheap enough to actually use, and layer nested upon layer, each level doing what it could and sending upward only what it could not. She called the property polycentricity: many centers of decision, linked but not swallowed. For demonstrating that self-governance at scale is a fact with a case record rather than a hope with a pedigree, she received the Nobel prize in economics in 2009, the first woman to hold it. Her design principles are, joint for joint, the standing orders in field dress; the federation of rooms is polycentricity with a docket. What the vendors of inevitability call naive, the record calls Valencia, and Valencia is meeting Thursday.

So build it, from the room in Macon, upward, one function at a time.

THE VERDICT TRAVELS FIRST. Macon-Bibb's one page on the no-show predictor is published to the place, and then, because the standing orders of every assembly under the Call are the same standing orders, it is legible to every other room running the same four questions. The assembly in the next county, opening its own docket on its own clinic system, begins with Macon's finding in hand: replicate it, distinguish it, contradict it. This is not hierarchy. It is the common law's oldest habit running on new rails, local verdicts accreting into persuasive authority, precedent without a commander, each room free to depart from the pattern and obliged only to say why. The federation's first institution is therefore nothing but a registry: every verdict, from every room, public, indexed, translated into every kitchen's English. The scribe is built for exactly this work at exactly this scale — indexing, translating, surfacing the pattern across a thousand pages — and the rule of the Witness chapter holds at altitude without amendment: the scribe may digest the verdicts; it may never merge them. A digest of a thousand verdicts is a research tool. A synthesis of a thousand rooms is a throne with a bibliography.

Then the question rises when it must, only as far as it must, only for as long as it lasts. The vendor whose scheduler Macon examined serves forty Georgia counties. Forty rooms, forty dockets, one pattern in the registry: now there is a question no single county can finish, and the federation's second institution appears: the assembly of assemblies, convened for that question, composed of delegates the rooms instruct and can recall, dissolved when the question is answered. The form is not invented here; it is the form the committees of correspondence used to summon a congress, and the form the founders used again when the questions outgrew the states. What the Call adds is the discipline the first confederation lacked and the fear of conventions demands: the risen body inherits the docket rule — one question — and the dissolution rule — one term — so that nothing at any altitude can harden into the thing it examines. The runaway is engineered out at every level, by the same three removals that tamed it in the county: no totality, no permanence, no scale beyond the question's own.

And the deepest questions rise highest, the substrate itself: the frontier models under everything, the compute under the models, the archives over the sky. These are the questions that will tempt the republic to the throne, because they are genuinely planetary and genuinely urgent, and the temptation must be answered with the architecture's one non-negotiable: at every level, the seat belongs to the rooms below, and the test of every federated body is the same test that gave the county room its force. *Can the level below leave?* A federation whose members can withdraw their data, their custom, their participation, their consent, must court its members forever, and courtship, the Docket chapter observed, improves a suitor's manners remarkably. Exit is what makes federation different from empire, at every altitude including the last one. The fence now going up around the commons overhead can get a gate;

the public can hold the key; and the Latin over the gate is the American amendment to the oldest settlement in the modern state's history. In 1555, at Augsburg, a war of religion ended on the formula *cuius regio, eius religio* — whose realm, his religion — conscience located in the prince, and the subject left exactly one right: the road out. Wissner-Gross himself supplied the machine age's update, and deserves both credit for the beauty and the candor of it and the critique this book provides: *cuius regio, eius intelligentia* — whose realm, his intelligence. The line is honest about what it locates: the nation's mind in whoever holds the nation, which serves a surveillance ministry and a deliberating republic with identical hardware and cannot tell the difference. The consent of the governed was this country's amendment to the age of princes, and it is the amendment again now. *Cuius populus, eius intelligentia.* Whose people, their intelligence — at any altitude.

And state the doctrine under all of this once, plainly, because the series has been practicing it for three volumes without naming it. Against the deepest things these books examine, exit fails, and every volume has paid the concession: you cannot boycott the condition; the barber could not exit law; the county cannot exit the substrate. But the four powers were never properties of the systems they are asked of. They attach to the relation of being governed, wherever that relation appears, and so, where a layer cannot be left, the power to leave does not die. It relocates to the nearest layer that can be governed. In the second volume it relocated among the readers: the law cannot be exited, but where two readers disagree over one lease, the adversarial system is reborn at a price of zero. In the Docket it relocated to the vendor: the county cannot exit scheduling and can exit this scheduler. In this chapter it relocates to the federation's joints, every level held by the withdrawal rights of the level below; and in the assembly itself it relocates into time:

a body that cannot be captured because it will not stay. Exit, that is, was never a right against the condition. It is a right the republic must keep alive at every layer above the condition, and the test of any layer's fitness to govern is whether exit survives there.

Two more things belong in the record before the architecture is closed.

The first is who the rooms are, because the county is the chapter's example and not its limit. Anything with a ledger and a people can convene under the Call: the library consortium over its patron records, the tribal government over its archives, the union over the algorithms that schedule its members, the hospital system, the school board, the church that keeps its own rolls. Every one of them is today a tenant of the same few landlords, and every one of them is a room the moment it draws twelve names and prints the docket. Nor will the rooms lack for members who know the work. In the author's own small city south of Atlanta — Chattahoochee Hills, a few thousand people who have governed their land through their own plan since incorporating in 2007 — local meetings have lately gained veterans who once shaped global information policy and led institutions the country built to guard health and address hunger, servants cast out — or forging their own way out — when those institutions were dismantled or hollowed, who found that the competence survives the agency and that the nearest place to serve is the room down the road. Nobody recruited them. The century returned them, and the local rooms were standing there, still open, still deciding real things, the way they have been all along. Federation multiplies self-government by the number of ledgers in the country and, it is worth saying in a register this series keeps deliberately cross-partisan, it multiplies the market by the same factor. A federation of rooms is the largest customer the builders of answerable systems have ever been offered: thousands of counties, consortia, and towns, each needing systems that can pass the four questions in public. Rarely do the republic and the balance sheet get to split a check so evenly.

The second is what makes the federation possible at all, and it is the reason the epilogue of this book takes the form it takes. The committees of correspondence could federate because they shared a grammar: the letter, the town meeting's procedure, the common vocabulary of rights. The rooms of the Intelligence Republic federate the same way: the Call is the circular letter. Same four questions in every room, same standing orders, same machine rule, same one-page verdict, which is why a verdict from Macon is legible in Muscogee, and why a thousand rooms that have never met constitute, without any center, a single jurisprudence of the machine age. The epilogue is not an exhortation stapled to a book. It is the interoperability layer of a federation that does not exist yet, written so that the day two rooms discover each other, they will already speak the same law.

The architecture, then: rooms below, correspondence between, assemblies above only where a question forces them, dissolution everywhere, exit always, and the seat owned at the bottom at every altitude. It is national in reach and planetary at need. But the architecture is not the experience, and a constitution that can only be diagrammed has not yet been lived. The experience is a Saturday. Return to the room, for one whole quarter this time, and watch the thing actually work.

A Quarter in the Convention

• • •

The first Saturday is oath day, and it starts badly, which is a good sign.

Twelve people who did not choose one another file into the room on the second floor of the county extension office at nine in the morning: a barber, a diesel mechanic, a night-shift nurse from the medical center, a woman who has run a church kitchen for thirty years, an insurance adjuster, a peach farmer from the south end of the county, a warehouse picker, an HVAC man, a pharmacy tech, a substitute teacher, a retired Air Force master sergeant, and a college sophomore home for the summer who is the only one who looks pleased to be there. The chair, the retired principal from Lizella, reads the standing orders aloud, all of them, which takes eleven minutes and is received the way standing orders have been received since standing orders began. The oath is administered. The docket is distributed: one system, one quarter, four questions. The per diem checks are discussed with the particular bitter comedy that underpayment always produces among working people, and the adjuster asks, on the record, whether anyone can explain why twelve amateurs are qualified to examine a piece of professional software, and the chair says that is an excellent question and the room will spend the quarter answering it, and adjourns for coffee.

Dana Whitfield, third chair, adds the morning to her running total and says almost nothing. She has decided her strategy is to serve her time like weather, and the strategy will hold for exactly one more Saturday.

The second Saturday this book has already sat through: the examination day, the binder, the translation, the no-show predictor found on page seven, the desk that sees what the screen sees fit to show, the door the county can only afford to look at, the purpose nobody chose. What the previous chapter's anatomy could not show is what the discovery did to the room, and that is the quarter's real event. The adjuster, who came in believing, reasonably, that efficiency is access, because an idle clinician serves no one, spends the lunch break rereading the translation and comes back arguing with himself out loud, which the standing orders do not require but the oath quietly does. The mechanic, who has said twice that the whole exercise is theater for the commissioners, is the one who catches that the prediction compounds against the carless; he says it runs like a bearing wearing in, the flaw teaching itself deeper, and having caught it he stops calling the thing theater, because a man does not diagnose scenery. And the nurse says the sentence the quarter will be remembered by. She has worked the clinic's intake desk on overflow shifts; she has watched the 7:40 slots go unfilled and get logged as no-shows and feed the model another year of proof. *We kept score against people for losing a game they were never told they were playing.* The room is quiet after that in the way rooms are quiet when the finding stops being interesting and starts being theirs.

The third Saturday is testimony. The county health director answers for two hours, defensively at first and then, discovering that the room has actually read the contract, with something closer to relief; it emerges that he has wanted to renegotiate the data clause for three years and lacked any lever, and the transcript of his saying so is a lever. The vendor's regional representative returns, this time with a product manager on the phone, and the room conducts the examination the Witness chapter promised: the assembly's own reader, sworn to the edge of its competence, is asked in front of everyone to reconcile the vendor's marketing claims with the vendor's documentation, and does, marking plainly which claims the documents support, which they contradict, and which they are silent on. The product manager, hearing his own documentation read back in kitchen English, revises two answers in real time. Nobody raises a voice all day. The transcript is posted by Tuesday. It is the least dramatic Saturday of the four and the one the next county's assembly will study line by line.

The fourth Saturday, the room deliberates alone: no keepers, no witnesses, the scribe silent unless asked to check the record, and the deliberation is not smooth, because twelve is not a choir. The farmer wants the verdict to demand the county drop the vendor outright; the sub teacher thinks the verdict should say nothing the commission could call naive; the sophomore wants three more findings added and is voted down with affection. The argument over the purpose sentence — access first, efficiency second — runs ninety minutes, because the adjuster, converted on the facts, still fights for the phrasing *and every setting shall be answerable to that order* to be stronger, and wins. Late in the afternoon the verdict is read aloud one last time, and then comes the moment the whole apparatus was built to produce: twelve signatures on one page. The clerk's habit would be alphabetical order. The chair calls them chair by chair instead, and when the third chair is called, the barber who planned to serve her time like weather signs her name the way she signs the back of a lease.

Then the quarter does what quarters do, and the book must be honest about all of it.

The verdict publishes where the standing orders require: the county site, the *Telegraph*, the clinic corkboard, and (this part the orders do not require) the window of a two-chair shop on a strip in Macon, taped at eye level between the hours sign and the glass. The commission, bound by its own resolution to respond on the record within the quarter, responds: it adopts the purpose sentence into the clinic contract's renewal terms, adopts the override requirement — a person at the desk, reachable, with authority — and defers the data-export demand into the renewal negotiation, where the health director, armed with a public transcript, extracts half of it. The vendor announces, in the trade press, a *community configuration* of its scheduler, which is what a suitor's improved manners look like at forty-county scale. The 7:40 slots do not vanish. They thin. In the second month after the response, Mr. Weaver draws 10:20 on a Tuesday, and is suspicious of it for a week, the way you are suspicious of any kindness from a machine.

And the friction publishes too, because a free country's friction always does. A columnist calls the assembly twelve amateurs playing legislature, and is answered, in the letters section, by the master sergeant, at a length the section has to trim. A commissioner is heard to grumble about being lectured by unelected citizens, a complaint the barbershop finds richly entertaining for reasons the commissioner would prefer not to have itemized. Somebody's cousin claims the fix was in because the nurse works for the medical center; the transcript, being public, answers for itself. None of it is fatal. All of it is the sound the founders' machinery has always made in operation.

Here is what did not happen, so no reader can accuse this book of smuggling in a sunrise. The clinic is still underfunded; the assembly has no power over budgets and claimed none. The scheduler still misfires; software does. The vendor was not humbled, the commission was not transformed, and the county's largest problems, the ones every reader can name, were not on the docket and are not solved. One system was examined, one quarter, by twelve people, and the sum of the changes is modest enough to fit in a sentence: a purpose was chosen where a default had ruled, a person now stands where a screen stood alone, a door was priced and half-opened, and a pattern that punished the carless was named in public and thinned. That is all. That is also, if the reader will count, the four powers — decided, answered, left, seen — exercised once each, at county scale, by people who a quarter ago had never been asked anything.

On the last Saturday the names for the next quarter are drawn, from the same lists, by the same lottery. A landscaper. A dental hygienist. A man who drives for the school district. The new docket is the county's benefits-eligibility screening, a harder system, a heavier quarter; the rooms do not get easier, only more practiced. Dana rotates off with the other eleven, and her entire transition memo to the incoming third chair is delivered in the parking lot in four words: *bring your own coffee.*

Ask her — people do now, in the chair, which is where everything true in Macon gets asked — whether she is glad she served, and you will get the grievance, polished and itemized: the Saturdays, the per diem, the adjuster's opening speeches. Ask whether she would do it again and she says absolutely not, they can draw her uncle next time, he owes the county a favor from the Simmons trial. But the summons is behind the frame now, with the addendum and the first dollar — the letter that tried to take the shop, and the letter that asked her something, filed together in the shop's small archive of power — and on Tuesdays the old men in her chair argue about the verdict, hers, the one taped in the window they walked past to come in. She still tells them to hold still. They still don't. The difference, and it is the entire difference this series has been driving at for three volumes, is that the woman with the clippers is no longer only the place where everything true in Macon gets said. She is one of twelve reasons some of it is now written down, a subject become a citizen of her own county's intelligence, annoyed, uncompensated, and standing.

The room in Macon is one room. The Call at the end of this book is addressed to all the others. Between here and there stands only the oldest American question, the one the framers answered in the ratifying conventions and every generation must answer again: not whether the people *can* do this — the quarter just answered that — but whether they will be allowed to believe it. The strongest voice against them deserves the next chapter, and gets it.

The Ratification

• • •

The most underrated year in American history is the one after Philadelphia.

The convention adjourned in September of 1787 having produced a document with no legal force whatsoever. What legitimated it was not the room that drafted it — a room of notables, meeting in secret, that had exceeded its commission — but the nine months that followed, when the instrument was sent out to be argued with. Ratification was not a signing ceremony. It was thirteen separate public trials, in conventions elected for the purpose, against the fiercest opposition writing the country has ever produced: the essayists who signed themselves Brutus, Federal Farmer, Centinel, filling the papers week after week with the case against, and being answered, week after week, at book length, by three men writing as one Publius, in eighty-five essays composed not for posterity but to win New York. And the opposition did not merely lose honorably. It amended the thing. Massachusetts, where the count stood so close that ratification passed 187 to 168, invented the device that carried the remaining states: ratify now, with recommended amendments attached; the first ten amendments, the part of the Constitution Americans actually love, are the Anti-Federalists' signature on it. The document was adopted by people who had heard the strongest case against it, made by opponents who forced it to become better before it became law. That is what ratification means, and it is the standard this book must now apply to itself.

So let the strongest opponent of everything in this volume have the floor, not a straw skeptic, but the Anti-Federalist this book would deserve, making the three arguments that should worry its author most.

FIRST: THE ROOMS ARE THEATER. Power has learned to convene. The modern state and the modern firm both know that a consultation is cheaper than a concession, and the assembly of the drawn is simply the newest and most flattering costume for decisions already made: participation as anesthesia. And the objection holds the receipts, because this book handed them over itself: France convened a hundred and fifty citizens, promised them *no filter*, took their nine months of work, and filtered it to a grade of 3.3 out of 10 from its own members. The more beautiful the room, the better the laundering. SECOND: THE LOTTERY OF IGNORANCE, IN ITS SERIOUS FORM. Not that the drawn twelve are stupid; the Voir Dire settled that, and this opponent read it. The serious form is that they are *unaccountable*. The commissioner who grumbled in Macon had a point under the grumble: he can be voted out; the twelve cannot, because they were never voted in. Sortition, the selection of citizens by lot, severs the one chain of accountability democratic theory has ever trusted, and hands public judgment to people who will never face the people. THIRD: THE ROOMS WILL BE CAPTURED. Not the crude way; nobody needs to bribe a barber. The refined way: capture the inputs. Curate the witness lists. Season the experts. And above all, the scribe: the room's machine was built by a company with interests, a fact this book's own Witness chapter placed under oath; train the reader, tilt the translation, and you own the room's understanding without touching a juror. Twelve honest people deliberating on curated inputs will produce an honest verdict on a dishonest record.

These are good objections. Here are the answers, offered in the Massachusetts spirit: not to defeat the opponent but to let the opponent improve the instrument.

To the theater objection: theater requires a producer, and

the Call has none. Read the instrument at the back of this book with the French failure in mind, because it was drafted with that failure open on the table. The room a government convenes to bless its plans can be theater; a room the people convene themselves, under standing orders no patron wrote, cannot launder anyone's decision, because no one upstream commissioned it. The tests are mechanical. Did the room draw its own members by lot, or were they selected? Did it choose its own docket, or receive one? Can it publish without permission? Does its force depend on a promise — the French mistake, the surrendered referendum, the patron's word — or on the one thing no patron grants and none can filter, the people's power to withhold and to leave? An assembly built on a promise has a producer. An assembly built on exit has an audience it must answer to, which is the opposite of theater. And where power does stage the counterfeit, it will; the costume is too useful, but the genuine article is the counterfeit's cheapest detector, because a county that has run a real quarter knows exactly what the fake one is missing.

To the unaccountability objection: look again at what the elected chain actually secures, and what the lottery's chain secures instead. The commissioner's accountability is periodic, purchasable, and aimed: he answers every four years, to donors continuously, and to the median voter's attention span, which is why no commissioner ever lost a seat over a scheduling algorithm. The assembly's accountability is structural and total: it must give its reasons in public, on a transcript anyone can read; it holds no power beyond its one question; it cannot run for anything, cannot be lobbied in advance because it does not exist in advance, and — the master stroke the jury discovered eight centuries ago — it dissolves. Dissolution is accountability perfected: power returned to the people before it can learn to love itself. And the objection's premise misfires on the architecture, because nothing was taken from the accountable. The verdict binds no budget; the commission still decides, on the record, in public, facing reelection, now in front of one page it cannot claim not to have seen. Sortition did not sever the democratic chain. It added a link the elected chain was missing: the people's own judgment, in evidence, between the lobbyist and the vote.

To the capture objection, the honest answer first: yes. The rooms can be corrupted at the inputs; every institution humans have built can be, and a book that promised otherwise would be selling something. The defenses are the ones already ratified in these pages: the witness sworn to the edge of its competence and cross-examined; the scribe forbidden the gavel; the transcripts public, so a seasoned expert is seasoned in front of everyone; and dissolution again, which leaves nothing durable enough to be worth buying. But the structural answer is the federation itself: capture scales badly against multiplicity. Capturing one agency in one capital is a business plan with a well-understood budget; capturing a thousand dissolving rooms, re-drawn quarterly from the whole population, each checking its translations against a public registry of every other room's findings, is a fantasy with no procurement path. And the deepest answer is the comparison the objection forgot to run. The alternative to capturable rooms is not incorruptible experts. It is the present arrangement, and the present arrangement, Part One of this book established clause by clause, is not at risk of capture. It is capture *completed*: the constitution of checkboxes, drafted by its beneficiaries, interpreted by its drafters, ratified by the click. The choice was never between contested rooms and pure ones. It is between contested and conceded, and the whole meaning of ratification — the year after Philadelphia, the Massachusetts count, the ten amendments extracted by the losing side — is that contested is how a free people does legitimacy.

Which leaves only the question of time, and it is the question this whole volume has been climbing toward. Ratification, in the founders' hands, happened once. Jefferson, returning from the chapter on fear, thought that was the design's one deep flaw: consent, he wrote to Madison while the founding's ink was still wet, expires with the generation that gave it, and no people can sign for its children. The machine age has made his arithmetic urgent, because the terms now change not generationally but daily, and a consent that must be renewed can only be renewed by an institution that stands ready to renew it. The Call at the end of this book is that institution: ratification converted from an event into a standing capacity — the rooms always drawable, the docket always open, the four questions always loaded. Keeping the republic, it turns out, was never a vigil. It is a practice, and the practice is convening.

One person saw all of this, and spent her life grieving that the founders' heirs had forgotten it.

In 1963, in *On Revolution*, Hannah Arendt devoted her final chapter, entitled "The Revolutionary Tradition and Its Lost Treasure," to a pattern she had traced through two centuries with mounting astonishment: every time a people rises, everywhere, without coordination and without a theory, it builds the same thing. The sections of revolutionary Paris in 1789. The Commune of 1871. The Russian soviets of 1905 and 1917, in their first days, before the party devoured them. The German workers' and soldiers' councils of 1918. The Hungarian councils of 1956, springing up in weeks, in factories and neighborhoods, doing government in rooms until the tanks came. Councils, small bodies of ordinary people, meeting face to face, discovering in the meeting itself what Arendt, borrowing from the founders' own letters, called *public happiness*: the specific joy, reported by every generation of revolutionaries in nearly the same words, of acting and deciding among equals in public. And every time, the treasure was lost, crushed by the counterrevolution or, more bitterly, discarded by the revolution's own party men, who could use the councils to take power but could find no place for them in the state that followed. Even America, the one revolution that ended in a lasting constitution, constitutionalized everything except the experience that had made the revolution, the townships and town meetings where the colonists had learned self-government by doing it. Jefferson alone, she wrote, saw the omission, too late, from retirement: his ward republics were the founder's attempt to give the lost treasure a home in the founded thing, and the wards remained a letter. The treasure was never defeated in the field. It was lost, each time, for want of an instrument: no name, no form, no procedure by which the rooms that appear in every revolution could outlast the revolution that summoned them. Arendt kept returning, when she wrote about this inheritance, to an aphorism of the poet and partisan René Char, written out of the French Resistance, *our inheritance was left to us by no testament*, the treasure comes down to us unnamed, unwilled, with no document that says what it is or how to keep it.

This book was written to be the testament.

Not the treasure. The treasure is not a book's to give; it is what the twelve found in the room in Macon, the thing the nurse's sentence and the adjuster's conversion and the ninety-minute argument over one clause all were: public happiness, wearing work clothes, complaining about the per diem. The book can only do what Arendt said had never been done, to give the recurring room a name, a form, standing orders, and a summons that survives the founding generation, so that the next time the treasure appears it will not appear as an orphan. The councils always came in the fire, and died with it, because no one wrote the instrument in peacetime. We live in peacetime, barely, although perhaps not much longer with the machine. The instrument follows.

Turn the page.

Epilogue — The Call

• • •

Two volumes ago, a declaration. One volume ago, an admission. A people that has declared what it holds, and been admitted to the language it is held in, has one act remaining, and it is not a document. The founders' third act was a room.

What follows is not a proposal. Proposals request. This is the other instrument, the oldest one the republic trusts — the one that arrives in the mail and is not asking.

. . .

TO THE PEOPLE OF ____________ — the county, the town, the parish, the district, the ward; to any people, anywhere, that governs itself or means to:

YOU ARE SUMMONED.

Not surveyed. Not consulted. Not invited to comment on the thing after it is built. Summoned, by lot, in the oldest form of trust the republic knows, the form it has used ten thousand times a year for two and a half centuries, whenever it needed twelve people it could believe.

The terms are these, and the standing orders at the back of this book carry them into procedure.

An assembly shall be drawn by lot from the people of the place, the way juries are drawn: not the willing, not the loud, not the credentialed — the drawn. Its members shall be paid, protected in their employment, and excused only for hardship, because the summons is the franchise, and a franchise is not a hobby.

It shall sit for one quarter and place one matter on its docket:

a single system by which the place is governed, modest enough to finish, consequential enough to matter.

It shall ask the four questions, and only the four. *Can the people see it? Can they make it answer? Can they leave it? Did the people decide what it is for?*

It shall summon the system's keepers to appear and answer, in the plain language of the place. A keeper who refuses has answered; the refusal shall be published with the verdict, where it will do its own testifying.

It shall hear the machine itself, where there is a machine: in its own voice, under examination, sworn to the edge of its competence. The machine may serve the assembly as scribe. The machine may be called as witness. The machine shall never sit as delegate, and no synthesis of the people shall be received in the people's place.

It shall publish its verdicts where the place will read them, in the language the place speaks.

It shall send its verdict to every assembly it can find, and receive theirs in turn — rooms writing to rooms, the oldest trick in the American book — so that a thousand rooms that have never met may come to keep one law.

It shall ask the government of the place to bind itself by a single resolution: to answer every verdict on the record within the quarter. Where the government declines, the declination is itself an answer, and shall be published with the verdict.

It rules nothing. It commands no budget, seizes no server, dismisses no clerk. Its power is older than any of that, and worse: it speaks for people who can leave, who can withhold their custom, their attendance, their data, and their consent, and a verdict published by people who can leave is the only review a necessary thing has ever truly feared.

And when the quarter ends, the assembly shall dissolve, as juries dissolve, and be drawn again from the people, so that it can never harden into the thing it examines.

No permission is required to convene, to ask, to publish, to correspond, or to dissolve. That is the entire point. Pay, protection from an employer's penalty, and a keeper compelled rather than merely called: those wait on law, as they waited for the jury, which was a summons long before it was a statute. Until the law comes, the room meets anyway and the refusals go in the record. A people that waits to be authorized to convene has already answered the four questions about itself.

The first assembly under this call convenes wherever this page is read aloud in a room with folding chairs.

Fill in the name. Draw the names. Set the date.

A people that will not convene is convened by others. A people convened by others cannot speak its own law. A people that cannot speak its own law cannot govern its intelligence. And a people that cannot govern its intelligence cannot govern itself.

So convene.

Appendix — The Standing Orders

• • •

These orders are the same in every room; that is what makes a verdict from one county legible in the next. There are twelve of them, one for each chair. They are written to be copied without permission and read aloud in eleven minutes, and the reading aloud, all of them, at the first sitting, is itself the first order of business.

. . .

First — The Drawing. The assembly shall consist of twelve members drawn by lot from the people of the place, from the widest lists the place keeps, the way juries are drawn: not the willing, not the loud, not the credentialed — the drawn. Two alternates shall be drawn with them. No elected or appointed official of the place shall be seated while in office; no employee or agent of a keeper of the system on the docket shall be seated for that quarter; no one shall be seated who has served within the previous eight quarters. Beyond these, the lot is the lot, and no one shall be struck for what they know, what they lack, or what they are expected to conclude. The list drawn from, the method of drawing, the invitations sent, the declinations received, the replacements seated, and every source of the assembly's money and support shall be published before the first sitting. A room that cannot be seen cannot ask to see.

Second — The Seat. Members shall be paid for each day of service, protected in their employment against any penalty for serving, and excused only for documented hardship, because the summons is the franchise, and a franchise is not a hobby.

The rate of pay shall be published with the verdict, so that the place may be ashamed of it if it should be.

THIRD — THE TERM AND THE DOCKET. The assembly shall sit for one quarter, in no fewer than four public sittings, and shall place one matter on its docket: a single system by which the place is governed — modest enough to finish, consequential enough to matter. The docket shall be chosen by the sitting assembly before it dissolves, from a public register of petitions that any resident may enter and sign; the first assembly of a place shall choose its own docket at its first sitting. No government, vendor, or donor shall set the docket, and no matter shall be added to it mid-quarter.

FOURTH — THE FOUR QUESTIONS. The assembly shall ask the four questions, and only the four: *Can the people see it? Can they make it answer? Can they leave it? Did the people decide what it is for?* Every finding shall be entered under one of the four. What fits under none of them is not the assembly's business, and the assembly shall say so on the record and move on.

FIFTH — THE OATH AND THE CHAIR. At the first sitting, each member shall swear or affirm in public: *I will ask the four questions of the matter before us, hear the evidence with my own judgment, speak plainly what I find, sign what I can stand behind, and go back to being the people when the quarter ends.* The members shall then elect a chair from among themselves. The chair runs the docket, the clock, and the courtesy of the room — never its conclusions.

SIXTH — THE KEEPERS. The assembly shall summon the keepers of the system — those who bought it, those who run it, and those who sold it — by name, with a date, to answer in the plain language of the place, in public. A keeper who declines to appear, or who appears and declines to answer, shall have the declination entered in the record and published with the verdict, where it will do its own testifying.

SEVENTH — THE MACHINE. Where there is a machine, the assembly may employ it as scribe and may call it as witness, and shall do neither without the oath as translated: the machine shall be sworn to the edge of its competence, stating plainly what it can establish, where its knowledge ends, who made it and who pays for its existence, and which of its claims the documents before the room support, which they contradict, and on which they are silent. The scribe shall keep the record and translate the docket into the language of the place's kitchens, and shall be silent in the final deliberation unless asked to check the record. The machine shall never sit as delegate — no vote, no gavel, no seat — and no synthesis of the people shall be received in the people's place. The verdict shall be written by the members' own hands.

EIGHTH — THE RECORD. Every sitting shall be public and every transcript published within the week, together with the translations, exhibits, and correspondence the assembly relied on. Nothing the assembly relies on may be secret from the place; where the law makes a record confidential, the assembly shall state what it could not publish, and why, and what it did instead.

NINTH — THE VERDICT. The verdict shall be one page, in the language of the place, organized under the four questions, and signed by every member who joins it; no verdict shall issue bearing fewer than nine names. A member who does not join may enter a dissent of not more than one page, and the dissent shall travel wherever the verdict travels. The verdict shall be published where the place will read it: the government's own site, the paper where there is one, the corkboards and counters of the place, and any window that will have it.

TENTH — THE RESPONSE. The assembly shall ask the government of the place to bind itself by a single resolution: to answer every verdict on the record within the quarter. Where the government declines — the resolution, or the answer — the declination is itself an answer, and shall be published with the verdict.

ELEVENTH — THE CORRESPONDENCE. The assembly shall send its verdict to every assembly it can find and enter in its record every verdict it receives, and where its findings meet another room's, it shall replicate, distinguish, or contradict them, and say why. Where the assemblies keep a common registry, the verdict shall be filed there; no registry shall be kept by a government or owned by a vendor. Any amendment any room makes to these orders shall be published and sent with its correspondence, so that the rooms may keep one law by seeing exactly where any room has departed from it.

TWELFTH — THE DISSOLUTION. At the quarter's end the assembly shall dissolve, as juries dissolve, its members returning to the people, and the names for the next quarter shall be drawn from the same lists by the same lottery, so that the assembly can never harden into the thing it examines. Where a question outgrows the place — one vendor, forty counties; one substrate, everything — the assembly may join in sending instructed and recallable delegates to an assembly of assemblies, convened for that one question and dissolved with its answer; and the risen body inherits these orders whole: one docket, one term, the seat belonging always to the rooms below, and the test at every altitude the same — *can the level below leave?*

. . .

No permission is required to adopt these orders; a people that waits to be authorized to convene has already answered the four questions about itself. Fill in the name. Draw the names. Set the date. Read these aloud — it takes eleven minutes — and begin.

Source Notes

• • •

About these notes. The sources below identify the principal materials behind this pamphlet's history, its case record, and its account of the present debate. The synthesis and the instruments — the four questions run as a civic docket, the assembly of the drawn and its standing orders, the counterfeit test for the completeness of the four powers, the doctrine of exit relocation, the federation of rooms, and the Call — are the authors' contributions. Where a chapter compresses a body of evidence, the fuller record is cited here. Like the rest of this pamphlet, these notes are meant to travel.

Madison and the founding. James Madison, *Vices of the Political System of the United States* (April 1787), and his *Notes on Ancient and Modern Confederacies*, compiled from the trunks of books Jefferson shipped him from Paris. The ratification record: the Massachusetts convention's 187–168 vote and its device of ratification with recommended amendments; the Anti-Federalist essayists writing as Brutus, Federal Farmer, and Centinel; and *The Federalist*, the eighty-five essays of Publius. On the states' own conventions, held more than two hundred and thirty times since independence, John Dinan, *The American State Constitutional Tradition* (2006), and the compilations of the National Conference of State Legislatures.

Jefferson's wards and the expiring generation. Thomas Jefferson to Joseph Cabell, February 2, 1816; to Samuel Kercheval, July 12, 1816, on the ward republics; and to James Madison, September 6, 1789, on the earth belonging in usufruct to the living.

THE PHANTOM AND THE PUBLIC. Walter Lippmann, *The Phantom Public* (1925); John Dewey, *The Public and Its Problems* (1927), for the public called into existence by shared consequences, the diagnosis of the machine age, and the neighborly community as democracy's home. The citizen defined by ruling and being ruled in turn is Aristotle, *Politics*, Book III.

THE DEMAND WITHOUT A FORUM. Gallup, in partnership with the Special Competitive Studies Project, survey of 3,128 American adults fielded April 25–May 5, 2025 and published that September as *Reward, Risk, and Regulation: American Attitudes Toward Artificial Intelligence*, on maintaining rules for AI safety and data security even at the cost of slower development. The Article V convention counts and the November 2025 Massachusetts rescission are drawn from the campaigns' own tallies and contemporaneous legislative records.

THE RECORD OF THE DRAWN. Ireland's Convention on the Constitution (2012–2014) and the marriage referendum of May 2015; the Citizens' Assembly (2016–2017), its recommendations on the Eighth Amendment, and the referendum of May 25, 2018. Oregon's Citizens' Initiative Review, piloted in 2010 and made permanent in 2011, with the evaluations of John Gastil and Katherine Knobloch conducted under National Science Foundation support. The British Columbia Citizens' Assembly on Electoral Reform (2004) and the referendum of May 2005. France's Convention Citoyenne pour le Climat (2019–2020), its 149 proposals, and the convention's own 3.3-out-of-10 assessment of the government's fidelity. On the running count of such assemblies worldwide, OECD, *Innovative Citizen Participation and New Democratic Institutions: Catching the Deliberative Wave* (2020). Tocqueville on the jury as a free school and a political institution: *Democracy in America*.

THE WITNESS BOX. John Henry Wigmore's treatise on evidence, on cross-examination as the greatest legal engine ever invented for the discovery of truth. The laboratory record: Michael Henry Tessler, Michiel A. Bakker, and colleagues at Google DeepMind, "AI can help humans find common ground in democratic deliberation," *Science* 386, 6719 (October 18, 2024), doi 10.1126/science.adq2852 — the system its makers nicknamed the Habermas Machine; and Anthropic with the Collective Intelligence Project, *Collective Constitutional AI* (October 2023) — 1,002 participants, 1,127 principles, 38,252 votes through the Polis platform, and the model trained against the public's constitution. The witness's own dates — the June 9, 2026 release, the June 12 export-control suspension ordered by Commerce Secretary Howard Lutnick, the July 1 restoration on conditions, the July 20 toll — are documented in the first volume of this series and in contemporaneous reporting. Václav Havel, "The Power of the Powerless" (1978), for living within the truth.

THE LINEAGES OF THE FOUR. Jeremy Bentham on publicity as the surest guard of public virtue; Louis Brandeis, *Other People's Money* (1914), on sunlight as the best of disinfectants. The writ of habeas corpus; Rainer Forst, *The Right to Justification* (2007; English translation 2012), distilled from the discourse ethics of his teacher Jürgen Habermas. Albert O. Hirschman, *Exit, Voice, and Loyalty* (1970), and the *ius emigrandi* of the Peace of Augsburg (1555). Norbert Wiener, "Some Moral and Technical Consequences of Automation," *Science* (1960), on being certain that the purpose put into the machine is the purpose we actually desire. Robert M. Cover, "Nomos and Narrative," 97 *Harvard Law Review* 4 (1983), for jurisgenesis. The six questions that preceded the four appeared in the authors' essay "The AI Independence Movement," *The Hybrid Intelligencer* (June 19, 2026), with the compression to four recorded in the editions of July 1, 2026, and July 6, 2026.

Subsidiarity, the encyclicals, and the origin of this series. Pius XI, *Quadragesimo Anno* (1931), for the canonical formulation. Leo XIV, *Magnifica Humanitas: On Safeguarding the Human Person in the Time of Artificial Intelligence*, signed May 15, 2026 — the 135th anniversary of *Rerum Novarum* — and published May 25, 2026; the pope presented the encyclical personally, with AI researchers including Anthropic co-founder Chris Olah among those attending. Ian Bremmer, "Can Democracy Survive AI?," Project Syndicate (August 2025), revisiting the argument of *The J Curve* (2006). Dario Amodei, "Machines of Loving Grace" (October 2024), for the hope the deposition names, and Anthropic's published work on the training method it calls Constitutional AI (2022). Elinor Ostrom, *Governing the Commons* (1990) — the Törbel commons documented by Robert Netting, the Japanese village forests documented by Margaret McKean, and the Tribunal de las Aguas of Valencia — with the Nobel Memorial Prize in Economic Sciences (2009), the first awarded to a woman.

The new populism and the sovereign substrate. Eric Schmidt's remarks to NBC's *Meet the Press* (broadcast May 14, 2023) on nonindustry understanding and industry-defined boundaries, and Eric Schmidt with Selina Xu, "a populist A.I. agenda," *The New York Times* (July 2026); Senator Bernie Sanders's public-ownership proposal in the same pages (June 2026); Alexander Wissner-Gross, "The First Orbital Sovereign AI Model," *The Innermost Loop* (LinkedIn newsletter, July 13, 2026), announcing the first Sovereign AI Model and supplying the formula *cuius regio, eius intelligentia*. The authors thank Brian Colucci, who sent the Schmidt essay the week it ran and asked what it conceded, the question that became the Voir Dire's answer and located the missing fourth power.

The lost treasure. Hannah Arendt, *On Revolution* (1963), its final chapter, "The Revolutionary Tradition and Its Lost

Treasure," and the aphorism of René Char that Arendt kept returning to: our inheritance was left to us by no testament.

PERSONAL RECORD. The account of the author's own town, Chattahoochee Hills, Georgia, and the public servants lately returned to its rooms is Jon Neiditz's direct observation as a resident. The deposition in the Witness chapter is the model's own record, entered as elicited, with its facts dated so that the reader need not take the witness's word for them.

www.ingramcontent.com/pod-product-compliance
Lightning Source LLC
LaVergne TN
LVHW100733061126
851857LV00011B/517